Rural Beginnings

STORIES OF FARM LIFE AND LESSONS LEARNED ON THE LAND

PRODUCT OF U.S.A.

BY CECIL E. DARNELL

Margaret
Greatest thoughts—

Cecil E. Darnell

48th Class Reunion
Aug 3, 2002

Cecil E. Darnell
999 W. Dansville Road
Mason, MI 48854

ISBN 0-9653778-1-4 $19.95

DEDICATION

This collection is dedicated to Lillian Hart Darnell and people everywhere who are rural at heart. She has always been the glue that held things together. Sometimes she was a buffer between strong-willed people, as rural folks can be sometimes.

Her faith in the Almighty has touched each of us who have had contact with her. She has always used music as one of the threads woven into our family fabric that added strength and understanding to life's quilt.

Mother has always liked *Our Old Piano* because it was so close to us as a family. Music can be a part of life, wherever one may be in life. It has always been an important part of ours.

OUR OLD PIANO

It holds our family pictures, in that place against the wall,
Our dark old upright piano, so important to us all.
Still today the peace remains that only a hymn can bring,
Mother always played the songs the rest of us would sing.

Dad's bass voice would guide us, but not in any choir,
We sang at home with family, by the piano saved from fire.
While music helps in happy times, it is magic during grief.
That is why we meet and sing, even when the time is brief.

Every child learned different songs, while getting on in life,
The youngest learned the very most before she was a wife.
Those early hymns still seem the best to those who can discern,
The eldest knew the fewest songs, though he was the first to learn.

When it springs from deep within, music heals the soul,
We worship with a blended voice, as life extracts its toll.
We build the greatest churches where spiritual thoughts can grow,
But our worship place is any spot where we can let the gospel flow.

When our voices blend with love, there appears a certain grace,
With that old piano as our altar, it becomes a holy place.
Our music is our special glue that makes our pieces stay.
And when our voices blend each time, that is how we pray.

CONTENTS

THE HOME PLACE 1

The Old House
Suspended Suspense
Rocking Cold Feet
From the River to the Church
Remains of the Fire

OUR FAMILY 11

Quilt of Love
World War II
Picture This
Miss Tompkins
His Hands
Remembering
Dear Deer Experience
Family Things
Hymns, Hers and Harmony

FARM WORK AND CHORES 33

Chips from the Block
Planting Grass Seed
Not By Bread Alone
Talking Time
Picking Cucumbers
Threshing

TOOLS OF OUR TRADE 43

The Plowman
Hayloader
Manure Spreader
The Planter
Cloverine Salve

SEASONS 51

Winter Wonders
Ways of Winter
Flying Mud

BIRDS, BEES AND OTHER CRITTERS 61

Snakes
Which Came First ...?
King and Prince
Why Do I Feel So Friendly Toward Crickets?
Chickening Out

GOING TO TOWN 71

Movies on the Wall
Haircut
To Market, To Market
Celebration

ANOTHER TIME 81

"Let There Be Light and There Was Light ..."
Flowing Well
Treasures from Then
Good Connections
Our Telephone
Neighbor Roy
Hazens

INTRODUCTION

When I was younger and anyone would inquire about our location, the answer was: "Our farm is two miles north and a mile and a half east of Barryton." Mostly anyone who would ask would use Barryton as a known starting point.

As the world expanded, other starting points were used. "We are 11 miles north of Remus." In "olden times" everyone had heard of Remus Creamery Butter. For those even more remote, the farm was in Mecosta County, about in the middle of Michigan's lower peninsula in a triangle formed by Big Rapids, Mt. Pleasant and Clare.

Even today, I always act surprised if someone hasn't heard of Barryton, even though it is smaller now than it was then.

— Cecil E. Darnell

THE HOME PLACE

THE OLD HOUSE

There was a pitcher pump and a cast iron sink in one corner of the kitchen. The well was 18 feet deep. Wells were driven by hand in those days and it was easy to determine their depth. The sink had a drain pipe that went through the wall, stuck out of the side of the house about eight feet, and stopped there in mid air. Water coming out ran into the ground.

Water coming out of the pump got cold with very little pumping.

Around the end of that drain was a tiny universe. It was a great place to dig worms for fishing. Frogs would sometimes visit, and certain toads lived there all summer.

On another corner of the house was a cistern. This was a big stone wall tank below the ground, built to collect and store rainwater. Rainwater was the soft water used before water softeners. Soft water was harvested by using a pail that was fastened on to a long wooden handle.

There was a huge maple tree in front of the house, making it cool in summer. It was cold in winter too, and the maple didn't even need to help.

The pump and sink were the beginnings of our home comforts. The kerosene lamps gave us light. Wood stoves provided heat and the ability to cook.

There was an outhouse for relief.

In the winter, the wind came inside with us. Most of the snow stayed outside which was nice. Over time, many of these things changed. Perhaps this environment has changed more than we have.

SUSPENDED SUSPENSE

Our barn was actually two buildings connected together. The west half was build shortly after 1900 and the east half was built in the early 1940s. The roof on the west barn was a corrugated steel material, created in sheets about 2'x8'. This was a long lasting material, required little maintenance, and was a giant step from the days when water would drip down on us when we milked and it was raining.

I must have been about 11 years old when that one panel of roofing got caught by the wind, and was loosened so that it would swing up and down on the end when the wind blew. We all accepted the fact that if that panel wasn't nailed back down, it was going to blow off the barn ... and soon.

We didn't have any ladder that was long enough to reach the barn roof, nor did we have any member of the family who had any courage when high up. The roof on the east barn was sloping, and we could get up on that and could climb to the peak of the west barn, and look down on the sloping steel roof with the flapping panel. There was only that one panel that was loose.

After discussing the situation, there was one possible solution. Dad was big. I was little. He would tie a rope around me for support, I would climb down the sloping steel roof as he kept letting out a little more rope. His location was just over the peak where he could see everything, and could use the peak of the barn for the rope to slide over.

While the barn roof looked high from the ground, it seemed to be even higher from on top. With a hammer in one hand and nails in my pocket, dad played out the rope and eased me down the roof with the rope.

The closer to the edge of the barn I got, the less courage I had and the more insistent dad became, but he was on top of the barn while I was on the edge, at the end of my rope, if you will.

Scared, leaning into that rope for support, trying to drive those nails through the steel roofing with the hammer, that was when I learned what stress and frustration were. The only thing that protected me from complete failure was pounding the nails through the old holes at a different angle.

After finishing my task, dad slowly pulled me back up the slanted steel roof to the peak. When he got me back to the top of the barn he asked, "Were you scared?" "No," I said. Then he added, "Did you think I would drop you?" "No," I lied again.

For years I watched that roof panel, fearful that it would loosen again, requiring a repeat of the adventure.

Rocking Cold Feet

Michigan winters made those unheated upstairs bedrooms a childhood challenge at bedtime. Rocks could be heated on the stove, wrapped in towels at bedtime, and hurried upstairs before the rocks got too hot for the hands.

The heated rocks were most effective when pushed down where the feet could be warmed against them. Once the feet were warm, it was possible to go to sleep. There is something about cold feet that seems to prohibit comfortable sleeping. With luck, the rocks would still be warm until sleep arrived.

It was sometimes possible to read in bed, if there were batteries for the flashlight and it was kept under the covers so the folks didn't know you weren't sleeping. Once that small enclosure beneath the blankets was warmed, it was secure, a special place in the universe where no one could intrude.

What if there was need for a bathroom break? Forget it. Some things were just put off until morning. Once that special place was warmed, it was not endangered by unimportant things.

From the River to the Church

The Horr Store sits there on the corner ... the river flowing past it sometimes the only visible sign of life or movement to those going past. Some must stop or the store wouldn't still be open. Sometimes it doesn't seem in business then the next time it is seen there will be a light on ... or some other subtle form of life. The next time I'm in the area I'm going to go inside and buy something.

My parents were married in that stone house on the other side of the river more than half a century ago. Denslows lived there then. Mother mentioned that when Ruth and Jerome offered the use of their home for the wedding it was gratefully accepted.

Less than half a mile west is the church where Mom and Dad met for the first time. The Harts (my mother's maiden name) were active in the church. My dad and Albert Lee were in the area on Sunday so attended the church service. Dad and Al had been working in the woods, lumbering in Northern Michigan, but were between trips north when this transpired.

Dad sang bass. When the hymns were finished my mother's father went back to find out who had been singing bass. He was trying to start a quartet and had everything he needed but the bass. Thus he introduced his daughter to her future husband as they got together to sing. Albert Lee also married one of the Hart girls.

Today there are no buildings between the stone house and the church. There are a lot of stones on the south side of the road where the house and barn were located where my Darnell grandparents once lived. The buildings have fallen and disappeared, only the stones from the foundations remain.

My Darnell grandparents are buried in the cemetery just across the road from the church. From their current location they can gaze over the fence and see the property where they once lived. There are a number of earlier Darnells in that little cemetery with them so they are not lonely with family nearby.

As we walk through this hilly little piece of final resting place, Mother reads the names on the markers and shares memories of the people she once knew.

"The first time your dad and I sang together at a funeral it was for our neighbors' twins. It was so tragic when they fell through the ice. Your sister was two then. Your sister is buried next to your older brother who died before he was named, over by those tall cedar trees. I brought those trees from the farm when they were about a foot tall. Look at them now."

"The first time I ever saw a dead body was when they pulled the twins out of the water. They just simply walked onto a thin spot in he ice and went through. Their kids were a little older than we were. Our parents were friends with them."

"I knew some of these people when I went to school in Remus. Back then, country kids often stayed with a family in town so attending high school was possible. There were no busses then like there are today. Going from the one room country school to the high school was quite a change for a kid."

"I was always fascinated with airplanes. When we would hear a plane we would watch it from the first sound until it was completely out of sight."

"We put a 'for sale' sign on our cutter when we bought our first car. We grew up on the farm where Smiths live now."

"I don't like those artificial flowers by your dad's marker but they were put there by someone who loved him so we better leave them. So many people have commented on your dad's marker. The tree stump with the etchings of the horses on the top seems to make people remember him the way he would want."

"Larry Covert once preached at the church across the road."

"Many of the cemetery markers were handmade because of the extreme poverty during the Depression days."

Some personal memories start seeping into my mind as she talks ... Uncles Charlie and Cal when they backed up the pick-up against the electric fence so when the dog squirted on the wheel he would get a shock; when they dropped that fine copper wire from a coil around dad's neck and then on the electric fence. They then had the courage to tell him how funny he looked trying to get a hold on that fine wire to get it off himself.

Fire was a constant danger in the early years with the basic heating systems. A barn was lost to fire, then later a house. Dad carried an upright piano out of the burning house. Usually it would require several people to lift that much weight.

So many of the stories have been shared by enough different people so they carry a certain integrity. Those who were younger then are not today. The lucky ones are still around, or so we assume. Is it possible that those who have gone on are really the lucky ones?

It seems unreal that dad met mother, married her, and is buried all within an area covering so few acres. Is there something about the vibrations in the earth, or in the human mind, that connects folks to particular places?

How I wish the stories were better documented. Had we recorded these incidents of happiness and hardship, the history, the interesting personalities, then these documents for the living could really better capture the lessons learned by the experiences of those who went on before.

We seem to learn so much when it is too late to do much about it ... from the Horr Store to the Forest Hill Cemetery ...

REMAINS OF THE FIRE

Logically, I know the house is gone. What will it look like? As I cross the bridge, the idea that for most of my life, that house has been there. Just trying to picture the homestead without the house is difficult, since I have never seen the farm without the house. We moved there when I was four.

Leaving the blacktop and hitting the gravel road, the river is high in front of Hazens. Their barn is hanging on where many have given up to weather.

Passing the new little house, up the hill by Renshaws ... our line fence on the west end of the farm ... our barn is visible from here. Now the pole barn comes into view, the tank that once held gas for the tractor is standing ... farm implements wait in the back lot ... bottled gas hog at the side ... mail box ... driveway ... THE HOUSE IS GONE!

As I pull into the driveway, in my mind the dog barks, but only in my mind. He was in the fire. There are no dogs here now. The "beware of dog" sign in the yard is now an empty threat. Old Mike, the dedicated watchdog, is gone.

An orange fireman's glove is visible in the snow, laying there on a black charred board. A lifetime of memories, now nothing but burned boards ... a few pipes hold some form ... pieces of metal here and there ... total devastation. A small sled, there forever, will never carry a child down a hill again, sits half good and half burned away.

Crazily suspended on bent pipes, the cast iron bathtub stands in one corner of the basement. How very fortunate that no one was at home when the fire started. That would have been tragic. It would have certainly caused death. The whole thing went so quickly.

Last year, new cupboards, new dishwasher and stove were put into the house to make mother's life a little easier. The front porch was added and enclosed, providing another niche for keeping the outdoors and indoors separate. Now, all gone.

In the front of the house is the metal casting that was the frame from the back of the old upright piano. That piano belonged to my mother's mother. When dad and mom were first married, they had experienced another house fire.

With their first fire, dad had picked up that piano, and carried it out of the house. While that is impossible, sometimes impossible things happen in impossible situations. Dad wasn't there to save the piano this time. Perhaps death was treating him kindly when it called him earlier so that he didn't have to experience this fire.

Many times we had gathered around that piano, and praised the Almighty in song. It was part of our family fabric, and the old hymns pulled us closer to each other and to our Maker as well.

Collected in the bottom of the basement, the water heater, furnace, refrigerator, and various unidentified pieces of metal are spread about. The frame from one end of mother's sewing machine leans against the wall.

The stainless steel tank from a cream separator, charred toaster, Vernors bottle are snuggled together near the deep freeze, which lays catty-wompos across varied items from the back shed. What a mess. Mike was in the back shed.

Even in the snow covered mud, the tracks from where one of the fire engines got stuck is still visible. The emotional "hit" from the fire was different for everyone in the family. Mother, who lost the most, seemed most composed. She had a ratty old coat, the clothes she was wearing, and whatever she had in her purse.

The accumulation of her seventy years — cards, letters, photos, creations from grandchildren across the years — all gone with the fire and smoke ... except in her memory. Two of her children were born in that house, in the days before a hospital was used. Three of her children had never known another home until they became adults.

And the lesson learned? Life goes on. The hassle begins. The good news and the bad news, Mike was the only loss of life. What if that had happened in the night at a time when a half dozen grandchildren had been visiting ... ?

OUR FAMILY

Left to right: Cecil M. Darnell, Alice Darnell Sisco, Clarence Sisco, Tessie Wardell Darnell, Neil Darnell

QUILT OF LOVE

She made designs of hands and faces,
From bits of clothing from many places.
Each piece was trimmed to fit the next,
With thread and love, they were affixed.

She pushed and pulled and ironed the creases,
After neatly fitting all those pieces.
She stretched it tight upon the frame,
in one small corner, she placed her name.

Through winter snow and summer light,
She used her time, both day and night.
A memory from her youth still lingers,
As she worked her tools with aching fingers.

After all the work and time she spent,
She wrapped it up, it then was sent,
With self sewed through, within, without,
It was a gift of live, there is no doubt.

WORLD WAR II

... was a distant war, but it touched all of us in some way. We were determined to win.

While world ramifications were wasted on a kid, several uncles were in the military. Talk about these family members in their absence made it real ... perhaps more than real, as their letters came to us with parts missing.

Little American banners were available for display in windows to replace those loved ones in military service. Special gold banners marked the homes that would be forever empty where someone had been before.

As a people, we were united in the war effort ... we would win ... we would do everything in our power to make it happen ... from the youngest to the oldest ... richest to poorest ... weakest to strongest ... we were in it together.

We students took dimes and quarters to school to buy stamps, to be pasted into books. When these books were filled, they could be traded in for war bonds.

Victory gardens were planted to provide food for the family so that real crops would be available for those fighting the war.

All types of materials that were needed for the war effort were rationed on the home front. No cars were built – jeeps, airplanes, trucks and tanks replaced them in the factories, where women began filling in the empty work stations.

Milkweed pods were collected for life jackets. We got empty onion bags at school. Those of us living on farms filled these bags with milkweed pods, and lugged them back to school on the bus the next day. What a wonderful country where children could help and even our weeds were needed. High school senior class pictures from this period show many girls and few boys. Many young men dropped out of school and enlisted.

Paper and metals became items for recycling, hauled from basements, attics, areas where rusting machinery and equipment had been left when it was no longer needed ... until now.

Rationing stamps were required for those on the home front, shoes, sugar, gasoline, meat, tires ... anything needed for the war became scarce at home.

These shortages provided some with the opportunity to make money through something called the "black market." Those who did this were known, and were not popular among those who had banners in their windows, especially gold banners.

National pride was everywhere. The flag was respected and was the symbol which stood for what we believed, worked, collected, sacrificed, dedicated our lives to.

One night our family took a ride in our pickup truck. In the middle of a field, six miles south of our farm, was a tent city. It was well lighted, noise from the generators mixed with the strange noises within the fence. It was a prisoner of war camp. If the war is some place else, what are these prisoners doing here?

Labor for picking our sting beans was scarce. The prisoners were pressed into service. We took the pickup with a trailer to the camp, picked up a load of prisoners, took them and their guard back to the farm where they became bean pickers, of sorts. At the end of the day they were returned to their tent city.

The woods at the end of the field was used for those things that all people do, whether they have facilities or not. Several years later, I discovered a swastika carved into the smooth wood of one of our beech trees. That swastika marked that prisoner's presence in our woods for the next 30 years after he was gone ... becoming larger as the tree grew ... only to disappear recently during a logging operation.

Everyone was encouraged to write to friends and relatives in the military, even kids could write letters, especially if an adult had written out suggestions that required only copying. Those away from home needed to know that those at home were thinking about them.

When those in uniform came home to visit, it was a high happy time, all around. Family, friends and neighbors were notified and came to visit and find out all they could about how the war was really going. Often, those on leave would make civilian eyes get big when they told of the low prices they paid for items unavailable at home.

Some of those who went into the service during this period learned trades that would serve them in peacetime. One uncle who was close enough to action to repair holes blown in his ship. He never really recovered from his experiences.

Another uncle went into the service, and when the military found out about his talents, they decided he would be more valuable to the effort if he was at home working on the farm. Those who were working the farm thought his greatest contribution could be made through military involvement. War does not cure basic human shortcomings.

Finally, the war came to an end. It was either when our military personnel came home, when the prisoners left, or when that big beech tree, with the carved swastika, became lumber.

Forty years after the war, ten years after the beech tree was cut down, the following was experienced.

His uniform looked original. Only his shoes were not regulation. They were dark, muddied suede.

Between Memorial Day parades in two neighboring small towns, he slipped through the bar's back door ... had a shot of whisky ... and quickly left to march again.

His demeanor seemed to say, "My world was just. While today's world does not remember ... does not understand ... does not care ... I know my time was just."

Picture This

Mother wasn't very big, but she had a huge determination. She was the picture taker in our family. She had a feeling for events that should be captured on film, and placed in the ever-growing photo album she kept handy to show anyone who might be even remotely interested.

We were country folks. Even though we lived out on a farm, we were governed by the same laws that required all the other kids to go to school, even though this didn't seem fair at the time.

To get to school, and home again after, we had to ride a bus. In those days, the busses were blue and white, not the common yellow color of today. It was impossible to tell the color of the bus from the pictures, however, because the only photographs available were black and white anyway.

Since I was the oldest, and the first one to go to school, mother decided that she needed a picture of me getting on the bus. Recording such details seemed important to her. I wasn't comfortable having my mother out by the bus with her camera. If I was old enough to go to school, I was old enough not to have my mother out by the bus with me.

Several times we went out to the road and waited for the bus, she with her camera and me with my embarrassment. I was too quick for her. While she would try to take the picture, I would jump on the bus and be out of her sight before she could "click" me.

One day, after she had failed in her morning picture taking attempts, as the bus was slowing down to let me off in the afternoon, there beside our driveway was mother, her camera ready. I had to get off the bus so the driver could take the rest of the kids home. As I stepped off the bus, she snapped my picture.

While she never said anything about it, that was one of the early times she got her way by simply outsmarting me. That same technique worked for her many times throughout the years. She simply thought the situation through, then did what was required to get her way.

I would like to see that picture of me getting off the bus today. It was in one of her albums that burned up when the house was destroyed by flames.

MISS TOMPKINS

She was a tough old bird. She taught fifth grade, and had already terrorized two generations, and was working on her third when I got promoted to her class. I'm sure she had a first name, but I have no idea what it was. Everyone called her "Miss Tompkins," no matter how old they were.

She lived in a little house that was directly across the street from the school. The school was her life. Teaching fifth graders, whether they wanted to learn or not, was her avocation. In a different time, she might have been a military leader, or an absolute monarch. She had a "control factor" about her that was more imposing than her tiny size. Any student who didn't do as well as she expected, well, she took it personally.

Most of us were too frightened of her to want to make her feel bad. She didn't like comic books, even when they were hidden behind school books. She could remember when the earlier school, on the same location, had collapsed. Some of the older residents spoke of her heroic action when that school collapsed. She was credited with quick thinking, brave conduct, and with saving the lives of students by her quick action.

My gut feeling was that she had a nasty test prepared for her students, and didn't want anything to happen to them before she could inflict her challenge. She was decisive, and always right. There was no other consideration. Her ability to take a ruler to the hand of the unruly was known, and the technique was described by her past students to those who were preparing to enter her classroom for the first time.

She pursed her mouth when she used her ruler. Her students would be prepared for sixth grade, or else. My grades in fifth grade were the best that I ever had. The ultimate fear was to flunk her class and have to spend a second year with her. That was not a happy thought.

If she ever had a boyfriend, I never heard about it. It never seemed like she had any favorite students, it was never obvious. She intimidated everyone, boys and girls alike, equally.

If was a half century ago that I left her classroom and walked down the hall to the sixth grade. Since there is no danger of ever having to return to her classroom again, I'll finally admit the truth. I was very fortunate to have been in that classroom with Miss Tompkins for that single year.

His Hands

The enlarged knuckles on his crossed arthritic hands demanded the eye's attention. The hands, their final service was to wipe away spittle and drop the tissue into the waste basket. Now he is at peace, all pain erased.

Those hands served him well for many years. They held leather lines connected to huge teams of horses, serving as instruments of communication, reaching directly to the sensitivities of each animal.

Even now, the mind picture is vivid, the double-bit ax deeply imbedded in a block of wood ... the exposed edge growing sharper and sharper as those hands laid the file on the ax with precision ... then exchanging the file for the finishing stone to add that final finished edge that he wanted. His final test was to use the new edge to shave a few hairs off his arm ...

Pure power when they grabbed on to something, those same hands gentled instantly at the touch of a grandchild ... and they held the rifle steady when surprising a deer at some unbelievable distance.

Before the arthritis, that right hand would control a 12' bullwhip as it clipped a piece of grass, an inch at a time, held in a small boy's fingers. They agreed ahead of time, if the whip ever touched the boy there was a 50 cents pain reward. The hand never let the whip touch the boy, but he did fake it once just to get the 50 cents.

The boy collected, but the whipster knew it was a faked job. The fingers weren't red, and he knew just where that whip was going when he used it ... the whip would crack loudly and cut gently. He could pick a fly off the stallion with that whip and never touch the horse. It did make the stallion more nervous than it made the boy, however.

Those hands, so strong, so gentle, so dependable for so long, now released from their assignment ... at peace now, their purpose served.

REMEMBERING

Mostly, she remembers the things that worry her, and those rememberings may not be in any order, chronological or otherwise.

Older people will sometimes respond to the question, "How are you?" with the statement, "I am managing to keep body and soul together." To younger people, that response doesn't mean much. Maturity gives the comment meaning.

Fuzzy edges seep into human thoughts with the passage of time. As the body and mind reach a certain point, they begin to experiment, preparing for that separation of body and soul which is eventually going to happen.

The mind takes on the semblance of fishing from shore. Casting out, then pulling the bait slowly back through the submerged thoughts, ideas, memories, awaiting to see if any thoughts are responsive to the bait ... any thoughts that are hooked maybe from the present, or the depths of another time.

Aging can cause the mental catches to become hybrids, thoughts and memories of different times and places melded into an image unrelated to either the past or present. Always the angler is the only one who sees the game clearly. Others attempting to understand the shared vision find the picture clouded by their ability to see the distinct lines between yesterday and today.

Which vision is accurate? Both? Do we really know? Hybrid memories from a mature loved one can cloud the ability of younger people trying to understand. WHY is often asked, but there is no answer.

As the reservoir of thoughts deepens, the specifics become less vivid, more blended into a mixture of the old, the new, and the imagined.

Is there really a distinct difference between a dream and a nightmare; a real event and one wished for or imagined?

Since truths are different for everyone, if the maturing mind creates a memory that is different and ends better than what really happened, perhaps it is better for everyone to allow the best memory to become the final truth.

We have difficulty accepting the mental process of "body and soul" not staying together. We shouldn't allow it to bother us so much. Such happenings are simply practice sessions as the union of body and soul, which has held the two entities in place for a lifetime, prepare for their upcoming separation.

Dear Deer Experience

The dogs were circling the single doe when he happened on the scene. The unusual staccato of their barking first caught his attention. As one of the dogs would snap at her, she faced him, as nature intended. Animals have their natural protection. Deer run from their enemies. Members of the dog family group into packs to hunt.

Deer run. Dogs chase.

Sometimes nature's protective features bring forth unusual action. A mother deer may go nose to nose with a dog, rather than run, if her young are endangered.

This scene was simple, basic, and horrible to watch. When he first saw the dogs circling her, he didn't believe his eyes. Such an uncharacteristic scene is at first doubted.

But there they were, the dogs had chased her until she couldn't run any farther. Once she slowed her running, they began their circling, nipping, barking ... soon she would collapse and the dogs would have her throat until she could no longer hang on to her life.

Perhaps it was this kinship with his land that made him react, or it may have been a sense of empathy from the corporate structure where he had encountered that same circling, whatever the driving force, he picked up a ready club and attacked the dogs.

They did not welcome this intruder. He didn't care. His heart was pumping from seeing this, then getting emotionally caught up in it. He kept after the dogs until he had chased them away. At first they nearly turned on him, but something held them back, perhaps his intensity with the club, or maybe they too were tiring.

When they finally slunk out of sight into some nearby evergreens, the doe just collapsed from total exhaustion. He slowly walked up and looked down on her. She watched him, but didn't move. A slight quivering of her skin was the only movement from her, except for her heavy breathing and watching eyes.

He eased to the ground next to her. Slowly he reached out and touched her. She didn't flinch. He gently began rubbing her neck. As he rubbed and petted her, he talked to her in a low calm voice, as a mother might comfort a child. As he talked and petted, she relaxed and began regaining her strength. This quiet time, this returning from expected death, this reaching of two animals toward each other because of a mutual need is common with domestic animals. Wild animals are different.

After the passing of some 30 minutes, she seemed to be ready to try her legs. When he got up off the ground, she did the same. As he began walking, she fell in behind him, following step for step. He tried to chase her into the woods. She refused to leave him.

Needless to say, such a quick bonding between a wild animal and a human is almost unheard of. As he is thinking this, she continues to follow him, staying just behind his right leg. When he stopped, she stopped. When he continued, she stayed with him.

As he neared the farm buildings, his dog came running out toward them, barking his greeting. The doe looked at him, there was an instant eye-to-eye understanding. He seemed to release her from her bonding. He glanced toward the woods, as if giving her permission to return to her own.

She bounded away, leaving him to pet his dog. She waved her white tail as she returned to the wild. She left him changed. Emotional experiences always have some influence on those who share them.

FAMILY THINGS

Every family has at least one member who is interested in compiling a written history. It is likely a good thing that such "people histories" are created and passed on to those who follow. Putting together this type of study is not an easy task.

One of the toughest parts of such a family study is to get other members of the family to take it seriously enough so that they will provide their own group input. Why do it? It is easier to just ignore it. Let things take care of themselves.

Perhaps this is more important to me because I am one of those with the urge to do the history. This project began about 35 years ago. I worked on it for a time, and then got busy with other things. Recently, a cousin sent me a photograph of one of the older families. It was a wonderful picture. There were some people in it who are now deceased ... some are alive and well ... some I had known slightly while I was young ... but the facial expressions made the picture powerful.

There was a power in that photograph that reached out and touched me ... it touched me enough to push me back into the written family history project. Not surprisingly, relatives are still not breaking the doors down to get their units plugged into the overall scheme of things. My concern, I believe, is to provide something for the children who will trudge home from school while in early elementary school with the universal assignment, "Tell us where you came from."

Shouldn't our young be told about their history? I think so, but everyone doesn't feel as strongly as I do about it or I would have captured a great deal more information than I have thus far accumulated.

Little things come as surprises. As I was guessing at birth dates for one family of cousins, trying to guess at birth years, based on their age relationship with mine. When the actual birth dates became available, my estimates were every place ... one cousin who is older than I am is ten years older, my guess was that he was five years older ... and on his youngest brother, I was nearly ten years the other way.

Such errors can be reduced in magnitude if the research is carried out when folks are still around who can provide the memories that are closest to the situation.

I just recently learned that my granddad had some basic struggles. My paternal grandfather could not read or write. He grew up working the lumbering woods of Michigan, moving north as the white pines were harvested from the south to the Upper Peninsula, long before the Mackinac Bridge opened in the 1950s, connecting the two Michigan peninsulas.

Granddad could glance at a log and tell you how many board feet of lumber were in the log ... but he worked mightily to learn how to sign his name on the back of his check to cash it.

In earlier days, not being able to read and write was not as uncommon as it is today. Migrating people didn't place the same importance on education that stable populations seem to. Those who could not sign their name were often exposed to the indignity of placing an "X" on the back of their check and then having someone else who could write witness the "X" as the official signature.

Granddad finally learned how to sign his name and left the "X" behind. It was a proud accomplishment for him. He never did learn to drive, nor did he ever have a car. One of his brothers made his home with granddad for much of his life, and his brother had a car and provided family transportation ... and later, a grandson learned how to drive and spent time driving his grandfather and grandmother to places they needed to travel. Beyond work, this generation never did a great deal of traveling.

Along with what I recently learned about Granddad, it was only a couple of weeks ago that I learned that Clarence (Buck) Darnell was born at a lumbering camp in Antrim County. I think that is interesting, and I am certain that others will also be surprised by the discovery. How many other little stories are out there about the family?

Hymns, Hers and Harmony

Things that were important to her included her family, her church, and her music. We always sang together whenever we were at the same place at the same time. It was a healing habit.

She had met our dad because of music. Dad sang bass, and her father was trying to get a quartet started and he needed a bass singer. When that lumberjack visited a small country church, joined in the singing, there was a bass and a son-in-law in the same person.

Her church involvement included everything from part time organist to keeper of the scrapbook. She had taught all four of us to sing. From feedback, we were aware that she had spoken of her children from time to time. We knew many members of the small congregation from childhood (both ours and theirs), when we attended that same country church.

Mother had a birthday coming up. What could we get her? We decided to sing for her, at her church.

Arrangements were made. We didn't tell her. We told everyone else. When Mother arrived at church, she was lucky to find an empty seat. She looked around and saw so many people she recognized, many of them who did not regularly attend this church.

It didn't really register with her until the minister announced that a special presentation had been arranged for her birthday. We went forward and sang. In the old days, people didn't applaud in church. It is nice when they do.

This was not a tough audience. We were her children and we were singing for her.

After a couple of hymns, the congregation was into the program with us. When we invited mother to join us in the next song, she was really moved. So were we. The congregation was informed that she had taught us all how to sing. We appreciated it and hoped that everyone else did as well.

After the music, the church presented her with an award for some of the work she had done. That was nice, too.

Socialization following the service was especially cordial. It was one of those moments in life that could not be improved upon. It was pure emotion and appreciation. Everyone shared it along with that tiny little woman who had been preparing us for that for half a century.

Most of my stories are from my point of view because I know that best. However, because of this, some readers have come to believe that I am an only child. Not true! I have a brother and two sisters. When I was 20, my sister Audrey Ritt was 15, my brother Don was 10, and my sister Carol Ruppert was 5 years old.

It was this group, a bit more mature, that got together at the church that day when mother was so surprised. It was likely that the experience was more important to us than it was to anyone else, but it proved to be a positive memory for us.

Since my "rural beginnings" date back to the early years of the family, it isn't necessary to say that today Don has retired from the Michigan State Police and spends as much time as possible pulling and working with his draft horses, Audrey is now in business in several locations in Ann Arbor, and Carol is in the health care industry. All four of us have married exceptional people who have been able to either change, accept, or adjust values to permit getting on with our (some say) strong-willed family ways.

Picture the siblings as in their childhood. When I discuss some of these stories with others, they remember them a bit differently. Audrey, for example, remembers that I was able to get dad to make her milk the one cow that she could handle. She had to get up an hour earlier to milk that special cow, because it took her a lot of time to wash the odor of that task from her. She would not go to school smelling like the rest of we farmers.

Today, she still remembers this assignment as an unpleasant thing. Likely, it was tasks like this that made her what she is today. She doesn't remember being able to squeeze out a tear when she needed dad's support with something, but I can recall those timely tears.

Don was never a problem for anyone. Perhaps that is why he was attracted to law enforcement. The career fit him well and society is better for his involvement. When he was small he was always interested in horses. One evening when Don was eight or nine years old, we were working with the pulling horses.

Dad had three big rocks on a stone boat to practice his horses on. He had spiked a 2"x6" board across each end of the boat to keep the rocks from sliding off when the horses hit the load, as they did, to start the boat moving. I was hitching the eveners, dad was driving the horses, and Don came up behind the boat and leaned over with his hands on the 2"x6". When the horses started they slammed the rocks back, and cut the ends off two of his fingers on the corner of the board. That was a sad time at our house.

It is fitting and proper that Carol went into health care. She has always been a natural nurse. She ended up with every sick animal or bird on the farm and from those nearby. When she was small she was always rocking from one foot to the other. If she didn't have a cat to nurse back to health she was talking or asking questions.

Even before she started school she would visit the barn at milking time. Watching, talking, bouncing from one foot to the other, she would talk. I would tell her that if she was going to talk, then she had to learn something. "Say your ABCs, I would tell her." "'N help me," she would answer. And we worked on such assignments during the milking. The only way to get her to try milking was to tell her that the cats would like her if she would squirt milk at them. I suspect the cats liked her anyway.

While the others will remember differently, there is no doubt in my mind that my accounting is the true one.

FARM WORK AND CHORES

Cecil M. Darnell

CHIPS FROM THE BLOCK

First he would look the tree over, looking upward, he checked which side of the tree had the most branches. That high up weight on a tree will influence which way a tree will fall. Then he checked out everything within reach of the top of the tree when it fell.

After studying the tree and surrounding area, he then began to notch the tree. A notch at the bottom of a tree also has influence on where the tree will fall when it is cut.

The chips were always big when he notched a tree. He would swing the ax from way behind him. The ax would hit the tree at an angle. Since he was swinging downward, the edges of the notch slanted toward the ground. Chips 6" or 8" long were common. When the notch met his satisfaction, he would place the head of the ax into the notch, the direction the handle pointed was where the tree would fall.

When the tree was notched, we took the two-man crosscut saw and began cutting through the trunk of the tree, opposite the notch. As the saw neared the back of the notch, the tree would start to tip. Once the saw cut began to widen, we took the saw out of the tree and moved back away from the three.

Sometimes a falling tree would do nasty things. It could twist at the last minute, sometimes the bottom of the three would jump back when the limbs hit the ground, sometimes the cut would leave a little more tree to break on one side than on the other and that would cause a roll or a twist. Usually, everything went as planned, but we always prepared for the surprise.

Once the tree fell, the trimming and cleanup began. The branches provided cover for rabbits, the limbs gave us heat from the stove, the trunk was a source of building lumber.

Planting Grass Seed

We were a farm family. What that meant was that everyone was a part of the "making a living" machine. Each member of the family did what they could, based on age, size, weight, willingness and disposition.

We had one field, located on the other side of the swamp, that had questionable soil. While it was light dirt, it was a part of our farm. We continued to try different crops, hoping against hope that it would work better for some new crop than it ever had before for anything tried.

The field had been fertilized for years, sometimes by using the manure spreader, sometimes it was done directly by animals being pastured there. The man plowed the field; the boy, with three horses on a three section drag, worked it up for planting.

The sun was hot. The soil was hot. The boy was barefoot. When the horses stopped to rest, the soil quickly got hot on the feet. Mostly the boy kept the horses moving because when the drag turned up new dirt it was cooler on the feet. The horses didn't rest much during that task.

When the field was fitted, the crop was to be grass seed. The tiny seeds were spread around with a little device called a "broadcaster" or a seeder. This device was a small metal wheel with cleats to spread the seed, a canvass bag to hold the seed yet to be planted, and a little crank to be turned that made the wheel turn and throw (broadcast) the tiny seeds in every direction.

Two target poles were required for this planting process. One pole was located at each end of the field. Each time a pass across the field was made, the person planting walked toward that pole.

After each trip across the field, the pole was moved over about the height of the person operating the planter. The planter spread the seed about the same distance as the planter person was tall.

When my uncle came by and offered to help with the planting, his offer was accepted immediately. Dad explained the procedure to the new recruit, and my uncle finished the planting. There was a flaw in the explanation of the planting process. Dad told my uncle to move the target pole over about six feet each time he made a pass.

When the seeds started to sprout, there was a bare section of several inches between each section of grass. My uncle was six inches shorter than dad. When uncle moved the target poles over, he should have been instructed to move the pole over five and a half feet instead of six feet. The oversight didn't show up until the seed sprouted.

NOT BY BREAD ALONE

"Man cannot live by bread alone," or so we have heard. What that really means is that along with bread, some butter is needed to make it taste its best.

Butter has been around for a time. Butter churns decorate museums around the nation, and many of the different styles can be remembered by adults living today. Many adult museum visitors will recall having turned the crank on a butter churn, while visiting grandma on the farm.

Actually, the real butter struggle dates to my childhood a half century ago. It was then that oleo made its appearance for the first time. Farmers were not pleased. If their cream was not used to make butter, then they were hurting. As oleo (early margarine) gained some acceptance with the buying public, it became more of an irritant to the farmers. We were farmers at that time.

I had been assigned to crank the handle that turned the wooden paddles that stuck down into the cream, and eventually, after some cranking, converted that cream into butter and buttermilk. But there was more to it than that. There was a fierce pride in the products that were turned out by American farmers.

With that early oleo, the taste wasn't the big problem, the appearance was what turned people off on the product for a time. Early oleo was the color of lard, which didn't moisten the taste buds. Farmers fought to prohibit the manufacturers of oleo from coloring the new product to look like butter.

Those first containers of oleo were clear plastic type bags, that were flexible, allowing the oleo to be kneaded. In a small pocket, in one side of the plastic container, was a small amount of coloring.

That coloring could be kneaded through the oleo. Once the mixture was completely meshed, the oleo took on the color of butter. It was a serious challenge to get the color mixed evenly throughout the oleo.

Back in those days, there were no ads that implied the idea that "I can't believe it's not butter." It was an emotional issue, and the strong feelings lasted for years. When farmers are threatened, they can take an aggressive stance ... serving farmers' meals that do not include whole milk, real butter, eggs, beef, or other such staples can make them a touch testy.

Today, that early battle has been mostly forgotten. Oleo and butter share the shelves in the supermarket. The color is already mixed into the oleo, and it is ready to spread. The consumer can choose what spread is preferred by the family.

But if the taster is finely tuned, the eater will tell in a moment if the spread is "real" butter. Can you tell the difference?

Talking Time

The cows kept the barn warm. We named our cows, there was cow #1, cow #2, cow #3, with the names running to the exact same number as the cow herd at any particular time.

The winter path between the house and barn was narrow, hard to walk, uneven, and changing, depending on the weather, whatever had been across it to crush it, and a host of other forgotten factors. There was something about the atmosphere in the warm barn at wintertime, evening, milking time that encouraged what we would call today "quality time."

While the warmth was important, there was an intimacy in the barn during milking. The kerosene lantern hung on a rusty spike that had been driven into one of the hand hewn beams for that assignment. It was natural to keep the lantern high to cast light and shadow as far as possible.

The cows lived directly under the haymow. The hay served as good insulation when stacked high in early winter. There were only a couple of windows in the milking area. Only a smattering of light ever invaded this conclave.

When the milk began hitting the bottom of the galvanized bucket, squirt, squirt, squirt, as the hands got their coordination, the sound of warm milk hitting the metal pail in spurts soon changed as the milk accumulated in the bucket muffled the sound of the process. The fast movement of the new milk created a foam on the top of the fresh milk.

Once the milk was flowing, the mood was such that conversation was possible, even though the talkers couldn't see each other. Maybe it was the fact that the other person is out of sight that made it easy to talk. It was a time to talk about the important things. The things that were really concerns: life, education, girls, sports, farming, family, the Almighty, the future, the past, even plans for the evening when the chores were finished.

Where do people talk in this modern world — in front of a TV set? While some chores will ever be constants in life, that special environment that permitted conversation, while milking by hand in a cow-warmed barn, with a dim lantern hanging on a nail, in the middle of the winter, is gone forever. But it still exists in the mind.

PICKING CUCUMBERS

Those cucumbers grew after they were picked. I know they did. We would hurry to pick them so they would be small enough to be #1's when graded. The little green picky cukes were graded by a series of ever increasing slots, the most valuable were those tiny ones that dropped through the grid system first.

The smallest weighed the least, took up little space in the bag, and brought the highest price per pound. No matter how small they appeared when picked, by the time we got them to the pickle station, they seemed bigger when they went into the grader.

There is no good way to pick cukes. The only way is to bend over at the waist, reach down with the hands, snip them from the vine with the thumb, and put them in the bucket. Since the cukes are covered with dumb little pickers, it is wise to wear gloves when harvesting them.

When it is time to pick cukes, the weather is really better for swimming than it is for field work. However, we picked because that was the arrangement at our house. If one wanted to eat, it was required that each one participate in the farming process.

Just as soon as the picking was done, we would take the cucumbers downtown to the pickle station to sell them. From the picking pails, they were dumped into burlap bags for transport.

It is called a cucumber when it is growing, when it is picked and sold, and it becomes a pickle after it has been "pickled" or flavored and preserved in some way. There were huge wooden vats at the pickle station. These vats held salt brine for preservation. After the cukes were graded and paid for they went into those preservation vats.

There was a walkway around the top of the vats where anyone interested could watch the pickles in the brine, if they wished to watch such a non-event.

The fresh picked cukes were first emptied out of the hauling bags onto a conveyor system. That belted device jiggled the cucumbers over the grading grid, only the most tiny fell through over the #1 basket ... most of ours always seemed to be #2's and #3's. Since cukes were purchased by "hundred weight" with the highest price paid for the smallest, it always seemed like they grew between the field and the grading place.

The pickle station is gone now. Even the tracks that carried the trains that hauled them out of town are history. The big vats are only a memory. There is a city park where the pickle station once was.

I'll bet those little cukes are still growing ...

THRESHING

Dutch Pitts still laughs about it. The threshing machine was at his farm. He lived a half mile south of us. In those days, it was common to "change work" with neighbors, especially at times when there was a lot of work to do in a short time. Threshing was one of those time intensive situations.

Getting the grain from the field to the thresher, getting the bundles into the machine, getting the grain from the machine into the grainary ... all tasks were demanding and immediate. Weather was always an important concern. The threshing machine was scheduled for another farm immediately after this job was finished.

At the time, I must have been 15 or 16, a strong farm boy. Dutch got me on the detail of carrying the bags of grain from the threshing machine into the storage area, where they were emptied and the empty bags returned to be refilled. When one bag was filled, there was a lever that moved the grain flow from one bag to the other. When there were several wagons filled with grain bundles waiting at the thresher, the grain came out of there awfully fast.

Young folks who didn't know what was happening were often nudged into carrying the grain. Being young, it was an assignment where youth could be used and a person could be beaten down physically. That happened to me. By the end of the day I could hardly walk, let alone carry anything. When I had the chance to pass this experience on to another person, it took on a lot more humor than when it happened to me personally. Dutch still finds my experience humorous yet today, forty-five years after the fact.

TOOLS OF OUR TRADE

THE PLOWMAN

The plow. A simple tool that has taken centuries to evolve. That extension of man that permits him to turn sod into workable dirt.

Deep within the chest of the horseman, very near the heart, there is a close connection between man and the plow. All other farm implements are important, but they do not hold that same spiritual power.

Perhaps it is because the plow is the first step ... or makes the greatest change ... or maybe it is a connection with other generations who have tilled the soil and planted seeds.

There is a distinct sound made as a steel plow point cuts its way through sod ... sand and stones punctuate the sound, but that steady cutting/tearing reaches out to long buried feelings, pulling them to the surface.

Other sounds hold certain comfort; the jingle of tug chains; leather against leather; horses hooves hitting the ground in a regular pattern; a grunt from a horse; a word or a sound from the horseman; all blend into one ... knotted lines behind the teamster ... he places one foot ahead of the other, time and again, in unison with his horses, and those who have gone before him ... both hands grasp the plow handles as they squirm to escape the callused fingers refusing to release them.

All become one as the green rolls over under the black. The complete unit, horses, harness, plow, driver ... all become a single entity as they go across the field ... leaving a new beginning with each step.

HAYLOADER

A ring on the end of a chain hanging down on the back of the haywagon was where it attached. A short rope was tied to a spring closed bolt that hooked the hay loader to that chain ring.

Two undisciplined small front wheels ran crazily over the edges of the windrow as the ground bumped and twisted. The larger rear wheels drove the wire fingers that picked up the hay and dropped it on the chain and rope driven wooden slats.

As the front wheels wiggled about, the drive wheels performed their assignment, the horizontal slats carried the hay up the back of the hayloader. As the hay reached the top of the loader, it dropped off on the back of the wagon.

With a three-tine fork, the load leveler would spread the hay around the wagon. When the load was completed, off to the barn and mow it went.

That ancient hayloader was another unrecognized step down the path of automation. Before the hay loader, the hay had to be pitched onto the wagon with a fork. At times like this...when we try to remember while trying to forget, that early automation is ancient now. So it goes with the passage of time.

Manure Spreader

It is a blue collar tool. The lack of respect it receives is in reverse proportion to the important role it plays in the daily scheme of things in any live animal operation.

How would anyone function with animals without a manure spreader? Can anyone remember? There was a time when the manure was pitched onto a flat rack, and then forked off again in the field. The introduction of the manure spreader automated part of this procedure.

Today, this unpretentious tool serves in a variety of ways in addition to original intent. Recently, early models began appearing as yard decorations. Sometimes they contain flowers, a sharp contrast with what they held during their working days. Rocks, at times huge ones, sometimes small white ones, are added to expand the dimensions of yard placements of these ancient spreaders.

Early rear wheels flexed muscular visions, with their deeply cleated drive needs. The implement salesman would state, "We will stand behind anything we sell except our manure spreaders," and everyone would laugh.

At last, the manure spreader is starting to receive some respect. Even the load it hauls is beginning to receive more acceptable references. It has become a "reusable resource," no matter what names have been applied to this fertilizer in earlier times.

Does this prove that science and technology can make a difference?

Remember, in those early days of power lines, when a farmer was hesitant about working under or around those electrical lines?

It has taken a couple of generations, but those earlier suspicions seem to have achieved some state of credibility today. In years past, the fear of the electrical lines and the product hauled in manure spreaders were considered one and the same.

Not so anymore. Both have changed.

Cecil M. Darnell and Lillian Hart,
1931, Weidman (MI) Celebration

Audrey Darnell, 1957

Back row L to R: Donald F. Darnell, Cecil M. Darnell, Cecil
E. Darnell. Front row L to R: Audrey K. Darnell Ritt, Lillian
Hart Darnell, Carol G. Darnell Ruppert. 1973

Cecil E. Darnell, 1954

Audrey K. Darnell Ritt, 1959

Donald F. Darnell, 1963

Carol G. Darnell Ruppert, 1969

THE PLANTER

The seat, seed buckets and wheels, imply a horse drawn planter.

Designed to push dirt on top of the seeds that were dropped just ahead of them, those split wheels had a specific assignment in the planting process. Sometimes this "quick cover" kept the seeds away from those ever alert birds that sensed "seeds being planted," much the same way they know when it is time to head south for the winter.

Before the use of chemicals against undesirable growth, crops were planted in "hills" so they could be cultivated both ways. Early on, a marker criss/crossed the field to establish where the hand planter should punch the seeds underground. When the horse drawn planter appeared, a check rower or wire knotted device was used to trip the seeds on a measured sequence.

Then it was learned that seeds could be planted closer together in a row, permitting the cultivation in a single direction. This changed the planter needs.

Finally, the cultivator gave way to chemicals. Today, there are hints appearing that some movement is underway toward a return to the cultivator, and away from chemicals. What will the future bring?

Exciting surprises ... of all kinds.

CLOVERINE SALVE

While walking through a pharmacy this week, I saw Cloverine Salve on one of the shelves. What a surprise to lean that it is still available. It has been about half a century since I sold it.

Along with a picture of a Red Ryder BB gun, on the back cover of the popular comic books of the time, there was an advertisement and a form to fill out to become a Cloverine sales person. The Red Ryder BB gun could be earned by selling lots of salve.

Cloverine Salve came by a dozen cans which fitted neatly into the mailing tube that carried them. While selling this well known product wasn't a tough sell, asking people to buy it was required to make it happen. Since it was a universal treatment for almost everything, every family needed something like it in the house.

One of my salve orders was in the mail box the day before one of the neighbors was having an auction sale. I took it to the auction and sold the entire order in half a day. The number of jobs available to a 10-year-old farm boy were limited, except working at home which didn't bring in spending money.

There were several ways to be compensated for salve sales. One could take money. There were a number of prizes that could be selected for salve sales. The smaller prizes could be selected for selling one tube of Cloverine. Other prizes were available for selling two tubes. The best prize, that Red Ryder BB gun required selling three tubes of Cloverine Salve.

The toughest part about getting the better prizes was resisting the smaller prizes when a tube was sold. I never had a Red Ryder BB gun. It was never possible for me to save my points for the big prize. I always had hope that it would work out, but it never did.

When did the selling of Cloverine Stop? While the beginning is remembered, the stopping doesn't even leave a memory twitch.

The first time I placed an order for Cloverine Salve, my purpose was to get one of those Red Ryder BB guns. The last time I placed an order was for that same reason. Every time I placed an order it was for that purpose and in my mind, "this time I will save my points until I can get it." Even now, after all this time, and seeing the Cloverine in the pharmacy, I wonder if that BB gun is still offered as a prize for selling the product.

Would I be able to save the points to reach the ultimate goal? Probably not. Old habits are hard to break. It would be more difficult to sell it today too, because it is not as well known today as it was then. Maybe it would sell well if one concentrated on senior citizens.

SEASONS

Winter Wonders

Cold of winter influenced many things. It required that ice be broken so the animals could get a drink. It made things freeze up ... cars, trucks, tractors, anything with a radiator that didn't contain antifreeze.

Pipes that were near an outside wall, wells that were not below the frost line, any substance that didn't contain some material that didn't bow to 32 degrees.

Severity of the cold could add a unique beauty to the surface of the earth. Wherever warm air escaped from a chimney, the contrast against the fierce blue sky was emphasized by the bright sun setting off the white against the blue.

Panes of glass, with one side toward the warmth of inside, the other side facing outside against the cold, would team up to create eye catching frosted designs on the glass. Again, when the sun shined on the streaked frost lined panes, an unforgettable beauty was displayed to the world.

Pieces of winter paint an earth that excels in its temporary state.

Frost turned electrical wires into parallel lines stretching across the land. Limbs and branches, covered with the shiny fingers of frost added a brilliant look to the winter woods.

Winter was the only time we could work in the cedar swamp. It was too muddy to work the rest of the year. Once the ground froze, it was no problem taking the horses in there, skidding posts, moving things around. It was a different place once the ground grew hard. The cold chased away the mosquitoes that were aggressive and plentiful during summer. Deer flies were either dead or hiding away until spring.

While most parts of the farm became more hostile in winter, the cedar swamp became more friendly.

Adding snow to the winter scene changed things. Suddenly there were all kinds of tracks proving that creatures of every kind were about. They left their tracks in the fresh snow. Rabbits were expected, but other tracks were plentiful. Some were larger. Many were small, some even beneath the surface of the snow.

Marks made by the tip feathers of some hunting bird left engravings in the snow where it had attacked some small animal and carried it off heavenward ... the feather marks separated from each other by nearly three feet of snow. What bird that hunts has a three-foot wingspan?

New white snow had the ability to change the earth. It could paint ugly dirty things snow white, it could fill holes, cover up dangers, make travel difficult, lubricate logs that rub together, make fresh cut trees slippery, and made it possible for the sleighs to glide wherever the horses take them. Changing from wheels to sleighs was a sure sign that winter had arrived.

Snow can cover too thin ice, making it dangerous for the unsuspecting. Snow can make travel with wheeled vehicles impossible.

Wheeled vehicles have changed for winter over the years. Once tires were nearly smooth. "Knobbies" were introduced, tires that had rubber knobs on them to give them more grip when driving through snow. Such a tire could throw the snow out from under the tires in an instant, leaving the car stranded on the snow high above any footing for the tires. Tire chains were used for icy winter travel. The chains would bite into the ice, giving the tires something to hang on to when travel was mandated across ice covered terrain.

Ways of Winter

Those "good old days" were not so hot,
With wood for fuel and a chamber pot,
Those who laud them are in a daze,
There never were those "good old days."

Warmth is a "love" emotion as well as a condition of comfort. People who love others want them to be warm. That warmth has not always been available by turning a thermostat. Something needs to be fastened to that control to make heat.

So many of the comforts we enjoy today have been available for only a glimpse in the story of humankind. A campfire by the lake in summer is nice, but depending on that same fire for heat in winter is a different theme. During the greater part of the last century most rural homes were heated by burning of wood. When we lived in a rural society, wood heat was convenient because almost every farm had a woodlot.

Getting that heat from the tree is a journey. On winter Saturday mornings we would harness the horses, hitch them to the sleighs, chain the tractor (with buzz saw on the front) to the rear of the sleigh, and head for the woods. The tractor would not go through the snow without that pull from the front.

Down the hill, over the crossways and up into the hardwoods. There was a certain quietness in those woods in the early days. After trimming up a couple of fallen trees, we'd pull the tractor up next to the box on the sleigh, and start cutting the poles into stove length pieces. Buzz-thump, buzz-thump, buzz-thumb, was soon a comforting rhythm between the man and the boy as the pieces were cut and thrown into the box.

While the sound of the tractor and saw destroyed the quiet of the woods, it did permit faster cutting of wood than did the old crosscut saw. (It seems that everything in life has a trade off.) With each buzz-thump, the coldness of the feet and fingers seemed to go away. The adage stating that "he who cuts his own wood is twice warmed by it" is true, except that adage misses several of those warmings that exist in the real life process.

When the wood was unloaded at the house, within carrying distance of the stove, the unloading and splitting adds another warming ignored by the adage. Those wood fueled memories are still warm, as are the echoes of the sound of the ax, along with the closeness of those moments that still push through time. The ax would hit the tree, and there would be a short time lapse before the echo returned to the ear. Maturity would eventually allow acceptance of the fact that light travels fast and sound travels slow and that is why the echo waited so long to be heard.

The warming of the house with wood carried with it certain chores that fell to those lowest on the pecking list. Carrying the wood into the house and the ashes out again, keeping enough kindling split to accommodate the morning fire lighting, having larger pieces available for "banking" the heating stove so it would not go out during the night, heating water for a bath is another story, but fell into the cluster of chores for country kids.

At our house, there was never any heat upstairs when we were growing up. Once grandchildren started sleeping there, heat was added. Those of us belonging to that cold generation that slept upstairs still shake our heads in wonder. There was a feeling of closeness and comfort up there once the body heat reached the covers, and the quilt could be pulled back from over the head. To help the body heat and the temperature of the room reach an accommodation, there were certain tools that assisted.

We used heated rocks wrapped in towels. Once heated, those rocks were shoved under those upstairs blankets. Working those rocks down under those covers with the feet was part of the

---

warming process. Diving in under those covers was one of those comfort moments from the "good old days" if there had been any such days.

One remembrance that seems so neat,
We'd all stay close to our source of heat,
And there were items, both day and night,
When all the world seemed cold and white.

And on one of those winter wood cutting trips, the man taught the boy how to climb a sapling, release the feet and let the weight of the body pull the sapling to the ground, giving one a slow graceful aching ride to the snow. Once the boy tried this on his own. Not paying attention, he selected a dead tree. When he kicked out his legs for that ride down, the tree broke into three pieces and he fell. That was the first time he ever had the wind knocked out of him.

There were other times when the procedure would change. Instead of us doing everything by ourselves, we would bring the wood up to the house before buzzing it to stove length. Then neighbors would come by and help us saw up the wood into stove size pieces.

There was a cider barrel in our basement. In the fall, we would pick apples and have them pressed. The cider was placed in that old wooden barrel. For a time, we would drink the cider. Eventually the taste would change and it wasn't nice to drink it anymore.

Once when there was a crew around buzzing wood, someone discovered that foul tasking fluid in that wooden barrel in the basement. Soon some caning jars appeared and folks were drinking that horrible tasting stuff and feeling very good about it. There has been very little thought about hard cider until a recent story in the *Wall Street Journal* addressing the subject of "hard cider" and the attention it is now receiving in the world of drinking things that make people feel happy for a time.

Most things change and change is good,
We no longer heat with wood,
But I'm not one to ever grouse,
Because I recall that old outhouse.

Nostalgia Through a Crescent

Cautious contact of skin with boards worn smooth by generations ... the universal position of thought and total equality of humankind. Sight, sound, smell and touch, stimulated after years of absence. Birds in a nearby apple tree; bees in the hollyhocks; flies as they have been throughout history.

"Library" changes, *Sears & Roebuck* failed via coated stock; *Grit* remains from the past, now months old, yet now read with great dedication ... science and technology from cob to roll. The mythical crescent is actually square.

Lack of snow at skin-wood contact point. The lengthy absence calls back memories, thoughts, dreams, ideas ... hope of youth, long since passed by reality.

Sitting on a piece of history, and a piece of kindling ready for the splitting ...

FLYING MUD

Almost in the geographical center of the 160-acre farm was the east crossways. This crossways was a built-up passage through the cedar swamp, high ground roadway connecting the front of the farm with the back field and hardwoods.

Midway through the swamp, the small spring-fed creek twisted its way under the crossways. On the east side of the road, the creek had been backed up a bit by the crossways. The water that had been detained had backed up enough to create a pond like appearance on the east side of the passageway.

The backed up creek water joined forces with the mucky swamp floor, making an interesting, yet undefined area of mud, solid road, swamp, cattails, pussy willows, frogs, and cedar trees of various sizes from brush to logs.

On the west side of the crossways, the creek twisted its lazy way through the cedars and swamp, until after another quarter mile, it slipped under the line fence, traveled another 50 feet, then joined forces with Chippewa Creek.

There was always a strange fascination in our minds about the creek. We could picture a large, clear water pond where all those cattails lived.

This area was a part of our farm pasture. Both cows and horses were permitted to visit the woods, drink from the creek, eat the surrounding greenery, and keep company with the deer that ran wild through the area.

We had run a "jump wire" from the barn, along the crossways, and electrified the fence that ran along the north side of the farm.

The "jump wire" was designed simply to carry electricity back to the far fence.

It was just wire, held high off the ground by an insulator every 50 or 60 feet. The wire was high enough to permit the cows and horses to walk under it, yet not so high it couldn't be reached by standing up in the back of the pickup.

The cows were usually careful when they drank from the creek, usually staying close to the crossways road. Sometime they would get out a bit farther, and get in the mud. When this happened, there was a lot of extra washing required before milking was possible. That mud was black, sticky, and abundant. We are talking about the days when animals might relieve themselves in the creek.

If this situation existed today, it is likely that the cows and horses would be required to be fenced out of the area, so only the deer could pee in the creek. So much for progress.

The horses took a different approach to drinking from the creek. Usually they kept their feet out of the water and just reached out with their long necks when they wanted a drink. Sometimes they would venture out a bit, but not usually.

It was a real surprise to discover one of the saddle horses caught in the mud one day. I didn't know there was a problem, but coming back from the field north of the swamp, there she was. She was down. I was a kid, and I was scared.

My first concern was to find Dad and let him know what the horse had done. He didn't appear as worried as I was, but I had seen the problem, he only knew what I could tell him. We headed for the creek. I was less frightened with Dad along. He always knew what to do in scary situations.

When we reached the creek, the mare was even deeper in the black mud than she had been before. At first, Dad tried to get the horse to lead out. She couldn't even try to get up. After several attempts to get the horse to help him, Dad decided that he would have to take a different approach.

After studying the situation, the "jump wire" running past, just above the mired mare, might be a part of the solution. After looking around, and discovering a loose piece of wire hanging on a nearby post, Dad reshaped the wire. He bent a hook into one end, and bent the other end so it would provide lots of contact with the horse.

After getting everything ready, Dad dropped that wire hook over the "jump wire." When that electricity came down the wire to that horse, stuck into that cold creek water, it was an exciting time.

That same horse that wouldn't help at all, was now showing enough initiative to get out of the creek all by itself. There was something about that invisible electricity running down that wire, touching that horse that was up to her belly in the cold water, that really made things happen. It was likely that getting the horse out of the creek took less than five seconds, once everything was ready.

That mare had been brown and white when she reached the creek. She was a strange mixture of a little brown, very little white, and an abundance of black and black spots when she exploded out of the creek. She threw enough mud and water so that even those watching were exposed to flying mud spots. It was a worthy ending to an emotional situation. The solution was so simple, looking back. Looking forward, it wasn't so clear.

BIRDS, BEES & OTHER CRITTERS

Tarig E. Zidan, Cecil E. Darnell's grandson

SNAKES

Putting up loose hay could be a dusty, dirty, clammy business. This was before the hayloader and side delivery rake. Hay was first put into tiny hay stacks called doodles.

During the hottest time of the year, hay is put up, when the sun is directly overhead, hay and chaff sticking to sweaty skin whenever exposed ....

Always big and powerful, the man approached everything with the intention of overwhelming it. Putting up hay was approached in that same manner.

His dislike of bees was only exceeded by his feeling toward snakes. There was never any explanation of his dislike for either the bees or the snakes.

He always tried to throw the entire hay doodle onto the wagon with a single motion. Most of us had to use several forkfuls to move a doodle from the ground to the wagon.

One day, when he plunged his three-tine fork into a hay doodle, grunted, and hoisted the hay toward the wagon, the little snakes started raining down on him.

While only six or eight inches long, those little grass snakes generated the same emotion of full grown rattlers. There must have been three dozen of the little rascals under that hay. He got 21 of them, and some had to have escaped.

The instant the first snake hit the ground and began slithering, the man dropped the hay, and started swinging the fork at those snakes, both real and imagined, and there were a lot of them for real.

When the last snake was either gone or dead, the man leaned on his fork, and panted as he caught his breath ... sweat dripping from brow and chin, his overalls soaked, the result of emotional exhaustion..

The boy never remembered any comments made about the snakes by the man. Yet, the destructive vigor of that hot haying day still remains as a strong memory. The snakes have long since shed their skins and disappeared. The man is gone as well. There are certainly no snakes where he is now, and likely only enough bees to pollinate the heavenly flowers.

WHICH CAME FIRST ...?

Every farm had a flock of chickens. They provided eggs, of course, and often also provided Sunday dinner. There was a special block of wood that was mostly reserved for chopping heads from chickens. Of all living creatures, the chicken resists death with the greatest determination.

With chickens also go roosters. Every rooster we had was mean. They would chase a boy whose only intent was to feed them some grain. Often the most aggressive rooster would move right to the dinner plate.

The flock of chickens was often permitted to roam at will, seeking food from the earth. Some of the things that chickens found tasty didn't impress picky people. Often the chickens would find the best picking alongside the road. Sometimes when cars went down the road the chickens didn't move out of the way quickly enough.

If you ran over someone's chicken, it was common courtesy to stop and notify the owner so they could salvage some food from the incident. A fresh killed chicken could be eaten. One that was discovered later could not.

Gathering the eggs was one of the farm chores that could be done either by grown-ups or by kids. Chickens could have their own personality, and some would willingly give up their eggs while others didn't take kindly to losing their eggs.

Have you ever had a broken egg in your pocket? Can you imagine what it might be like? Actually, a broken egg in a pocket is just as unpleasant as it sounds. There were certain things that were supposed to be done. Carrying eggs in a pocket wasn't one of the

---

things to do. But if Dad could carry eggs in a pocket with no problem, shouldn't a boy be able to accomplish the same thing?

No. It doesn't work that way. Eggs know who is carrying them. They are much stronger when they are in the pocket of an adult.

All the king's horses and all the king's men couldn't clean those pants ... let alone put anything back together again.

KING AND PRINCE

King and Prince were the only royalty in our family. A proud pair of Belgium bays, they just seemed to fit into our scheme of things for nearly two decades.

At 3,800 pounds, while their physical size didn't make them real heavyweights, their hearts would often make up the difference.

They just seemed to fit. They enjoyed showing off in harness ... going to a pulling contest ... pulling a wagon load of admirers ... or running through the barnyard with their shiny coats glistening in the sun. They enjoyed life, and we all enjoyed them. They were agreeable and easy to drive, quickly adjusting to the driver, whoever it might be.

They weren't always like that. As a young team, half brothers, they came to our farm from the farmer who raised and trained them. He had used them for pulling some big rocks out of his fields. He would shovel ... hook the team on ... and if they didn't roll it out, he would then shovel some more. Each time they didn't pull the rock, it became easier the next time.

Horses are sharp enough to pick up on this. They brought this training with them to our place.

Dad liked to take his team to pulling contests. Eventually, King and Prince enjoyed it as much as he did ... but those first few times required some retraining. They would go to the boat ... tighten the tugs ... back off and wait for Dad to "shovel some more dirt from around the rock." Pulling contests didn't work quite the same way. They never had a problem with a lot of those loads ... but they didn't pull them until they went back for their second hook.

As time went by, they got used to the different philosophy, and adjusted to it. Those early frustrations created some challenges for horses, driver, hookers alike.

As all matured and learned, those early days disappeared into a vague memory. This relearning by animals isn't that different from that required in our own lives. As we move through the computer age, if King and Prince could adjust and grow in their time, we should be able to do it, too, shouldn't we?

WHY DO I FEEL SO FRIENDLY TOWARD CRICKETS?

A half century ago, this farm boy was always looking for new ways to earn some extra money. One of the retired men in town told me he would give me a penny for each big healthy cricket I delivered to him. He was a fisherman and liked to use crickets for bait. The size and condition of the crickets available at the bait shop was not up to his expectations.

Crickets were everywhere on the farm, but I had never tried to catch any until this ready market became available. An old board just laying in the grass could hide dozens of crickets. When the board was moved, the crickets scatted in every direction, and they were quick. Crickets did not intend to get caught.

First efforts were disappointing. I would move a board, see 15 cents worth of crickets and only catch two cents worth, or even less. After giving thought to the situation, I found an empty bucket and cut the bottom out of it. Then when I moved a board, the bottomless bucket was plunked down surrounding the larger group of crickets. By holding the bucket tightly to the ground, the crickets were surrounded until they could be captured one at a time.

With practice, I did become quicker. By hand, the most effective technique was to get one hand ahead of the scooting cricket, then catching him from behind with the other hand. By using the bottomless bucket, the side helps with the catching by keeping them from getting away into the grass.

Experience taught me that crickets were often found in the chaff that fell between the wagon and the barn when hay and straw were unloaded. This became useful knowledge. By moving the chaff a little at a time, crickets could be captured singly by keeping them from slipping into the straw ahead of them. This source could be replenished on a daily basis. Where did they come from? I still hadn't figured where they went when they got away.

The crickets didn't jump very high, nor could they climb a wall at a 90 degree angle. This knowledge proved most useful. By digging holes several inches deep into the ground, and keeping the edges real straight, covering these holes with boards created a cricket trap. Throw a couple of handfuls of grass in the trap and the crickets didn't even try to crawl out until the boards were moved. This trap then held them much as the bucket trap did. This cut down on the number of escapees that were so discouraging in the early days.

As word got out about the big healthy crickets I delivered, other people started asking about crickets. It was a constant search for crickets. What a great day it was when I discovered a collection of cedar posts back by the swamp that had been peeled. The cedar bark was spread over a wide area, and that cedar bark was loaded with crickets. How many crickets can a 160-acre farm produce? I have no idea. With hindsight, I am sure I never endangered the cricket population.

I did sell a bunch of crickets from the time I was eight years old until I hit high school. That time influenced my attitude toward crickets. They are friendly creatures to me. They are welcome at my house. If one gets in, he can stay around without danger until I catch him and return him to the wild. I didn't do that in my younger days.

Chickening Out

Every rooster in with the flock of chickens was mean and nasty. I fed those chickens. Why would the roosters attack a kid when they didn't bother grown-ups?

"Because you ran—that is why they chased you," the adults would say.

Deep in my heart I knew it wasn't true. They always chased before I ran, or so it seemed when I tried to remember specifically what happened in what sequence.

"Why didn't you hit them with the pail?" they asked. "What pail?" I responded. "The one you were holding at arm's length behind you when you ran," they answered.

When the situation showed no sign of getting better with the passage of time, the man decided to get rid of the mean rooster.

"Which one was it?" he wanted to know. I showed him. That rooster bounced and flopped all over the yard before becoming still after the rifle shot.

But then another rooster chased as I ran. Another rooster died, and then another, and another until seven roosters had been eaten.

That last rooster chased me as well, but never paid the final price of the others. While I haven't been chased by a rooster for over 50 years, I still believe the rooster started chasing before I started running.

GOING TO TOWN

MOVIES ON THE WALL

Population in the small town never reached 500 except on Saturday night when there were free movies. Saturday nights were when the stores stayed open later to accommodate the farmers who came to town to do their shopping after the chores were done.

The small town was the center of commerce and communication in those days. A war was going on in another part of the world. TV was still unknown. Retail merchants provided the free movies to attract people to town. Folks coming together at the end of the work week became an important time in the lives of rural and small town citizens alike.

There were a number of things happening all at once during these Saturday night mixings. Produce from the country was sold to the townies and the country folks purchased or traded for things they could not make or grow themselves. It was a mutual accommodation that fit the times and the situation.

In a small room at the back of one of the stores, there was an informal meeting place. There were several chairs and everyone else sat on the floor, backs to the wall, once the chairs were taken. So much of the talk was of the war. Rumors and hearsay seemed to carry conversation along. Who has been inducted, who had been lost, what was happening at the front?

Once the light of day began to disappear, the excitement of the pending movie grew, at least for the young. Those who got to town early took the parking places that allowed them to see the movie from their cars. The rest sat on the ground or on whatever else was available or whatever they brought for that purpose. The movie was projected on the barbershop wall which had been painted white for the purpose.

Those movies served different purposes for different ages. When it rained there were no movies. Sometimes the younger kids would run around in front of the projector and get in trouble. Sometimes the older kids would sneak off by the grain elevator and grab a still lit cigarette butt for a puff.

Sometimes a boy would put his arm around a girl for the first time at the movie. The grown-ups didn't seem to take the movies as seriously as the younger folks did. As young folks noticed the opposite sex, the movies seemed to be less absorbing.

With the passage of time, the smaller towns of my youth have changed. As automobiles became more efficient, it was more common to go to larger towns for the shopping. The first big change in shopping habits was when some companies decided to have shopping hours on Sunday. Sunday shopping was judged by some severe critics in those early days. As people drove to larger centers for shopping, the smaller towns grew smaller.

In the days of the free shows, the annual celebration was big and important. The main street was closed. Car traffic was replaced by carnival rides, games of chance, and a frame of mind determined to enjoy the community celebration.

This truly was a celebration. At each end of Main Street, there was a place where those who chose could get a beer. Some of the more dedicated would move from thirst parlor to one at the other end of town, sharing good will with those they kept meeting who were doing the same.

But those days have edged into our history. The many small family farms have grown into huge operations under the management of few.

The small town has grown smaller. Where once two grocery stores worked well, one remains as a service. A multi-product party store quickly serves the needs of those who need gasoline, a few groceries, a pizza or a magazine. The drug store is gone. The dimestore is no more. The department store is a vague memory.

The bank is part of a larger organization. The school is part of a consolidated system. The grain elevator is closed. The pickle station has disappeared. Only one hardware remains. A skeleton of one auto dealership remains. The post office and the library are improved.

Those people who knew the town when it was a flourishing center of community are growing less and less in number each year. So sad the changes. So pleasing the memory. So different the present and the past. The people reflect the values of a different time.

Haircut

On Saturday night in a small Midwestern town, stores were open late. There was a free movie, projected on the outside wall of a big building, the forerunner of the drive-in theater, no doubt.

That was the night for the boy's first "bought" haircut. The barber shop was nearly filled when Dad and I entered, and only one barber was working.

The man started needling the barber, commenting on his speed and lack thereof. Soon those waiting picked up on the theme. This didn't put the barber in a real positive frame of mind. Finally, the barber got fed up with the hassle and said to Dad, "If you think this is so easy to do, there is an empty chair and clippers." Dad responded with, "Anybody should be able to cut hair."

"Will anyone be upset if I cut my boy's hair out of turn?" he asked. Since no one admitted that taking me out of turn would be a problem, I was motioned forward.

Dad lifted me up on the raiser which went across the top of the chair arms and was used for tiny folks. I sat. He cut. The people watched. The room was silent. When I was finished, one of those waiting in line said, "I'm up next." Dad then cut his hair.

Dad and the barber both cut hair until the shop was empty. The barber tried to pay for the help. Dad refused to take any money for his work. He had enjoyed the whole event too much to take anything.

What folks didn't know was that Dad had cut hair in the lumbering woods when he was still just a boy, and had actually been cutting hair for years, but never in a local barber shop.

This was the talk of the barber shop for a long time. Dad did accept a "light trim" from the barber in exchange for the help. They both had a good laugh out of the experience, and the barber was grateful for the help, after he got over his irritation for being set up.

To Market, To Market

It was the first major trip that I had ever taken with Dad. When one is nine years old, it is easy to get excited about such an adventure.

Loading the filled 55 gallon drums on the truck was the first challenge. Two planks were leaned up on the back of the truck to form a loading ramp. A big hay rope was fastened to the front of the rack. It went down and around the drum, then back to someone standing on the truck bed.

Three men worked at the loading. One on the rope, and one on each end of the barrel. They rolled the barrels up the inclined planks, while the man on the rope kept the barrel from rolling backward, and took some of the weight off the barrel men.

When the barrel reached the top of the planks. It would plunge toward the front of the truck, where it was tipped on end, and then slid into place. This procedure was repeated time and time again until the truck was fully loaded.

It seemed like we drove forever. We stopped and ate at a restaurant. When we finally got to our destination, we were quickly unloaded by a mechanical lift that was designed specifically for that purpose. Our return trip isn't even a memory.

We never got paid for that load of product, and it was the last load we ever delivered.

A synthetic product was developed, so our natural product was no longer needed for making the Premarin, an estrogen drug, taken by millions of women during menopause, and is used also to treat the symptoms of osteoporosis and heart disease.

Our product was urine collected from pregnant horses. Even today, this industry is still alive and well in Canada, but the market disappeared in the United States.

CELEBRATION

Celebration was a big doings back in those days. Main Street was closed, carnival rides and other concessions were set up in the closed area, and people came to town to celebrate.

What were people celebrating? Perhaps each person had a personal agenda, long before we used such terms. Perhaps the celebration was to honor another growing season on the neighboring farms. The kids celebrated because it was fun and fun was acceptable during celebration. This was decades before the Disney places, Six Flags concepts, or the Cedar Points of the world, so you know it was a long time ago.

The same year that I rode the tilt-a-whirl 13 times at celebration was the same year I kissed a girl for the first time. Celebration can be a distracting time.

We would have a lot of visits from family members during celebration. While our program didn't include fireworks like some of the larger places, we were proud of what we had, and we lived the experience with great enthusiasm and dedication.

Along with cousins from neighboring towns, people who had once lived in the community would return to enjoy the celebration and to say hello to old friends who would be on site for the occasion. Even people who didn't like each other before seemed to be happy to be friendly during these days ... former teachers, students, oil field workers, and others who had gone on to other jobs and places.

Celebrations seemed to have interests appealing to each age. The heavy tilt-a-whirl year immediately followed the younger days when novelty prizes were held in high esteem.

One year, the strong attraction was the little steam shovel wagon. One boy won a pocket knife one year. That knife was all the reinforcement the rest of us needed to keep on going back year after year ... "remember the knife?" ....

The daring rides followed, then the pounding machine, and the prizes won by throwing things followed apace. The grown-ups mostly talked.

A recent story about antiques included pictures of some of the items that people are collecting today. Imaging the surprise to see these new collector items include those carnival prizes. Those little painted plaster statue prizes that were taken for granted at celebration now have value.

Those little sailors with cocked hats, dogs, little plaster replicas of a number of famous people's faces, and near copies of other personages that were not authorized, but were used anyway.

The pounding machine would attract the macho men. They could swing a big hammer and sometimes ring a bell by whacking the rubber pad on the machine. It was mechanical then. Today they are electronic and have a lot of lights and sounds. In olden times, the only sound was the bell ringing, or the silence when it didn't.

There was always some controversy over the little wagon where the mysterious looking ladies told people about the future. This area always seemed to be a place of trouble. Folks complained about being overcharged, short-changed, robbed. It was a puzzlement why people kept going back there when there was always trouble, but they always did and there always was.

Strange faces on foreign faced dolls were to be hit with baseballs (and knocked cleanly off) and prizes won, much as today. An entire collection of games of chance/skill were there to keep parents busy while kids rode the merry-go-round, before it became a carousel. Ferris wheel, loop-o-plane, and whatever exotic idea was fresh and exciting at the time ... but always the tilt-o-whirl.

Sometimes there were girls around who were said to be doing some things that people wouldn't talk about. How could people know about such things if they didn't talk about them? Sometimes these things included sisters. Were some families just closer than others?

Always the thirst parlors did a thriving business. With one at each end of Main Street, the folks going from one to the other would always meet and exchange greetings as they traveled. Sometimes a straight mouthed spouse would wait for her husband outside the pub. It was understood there would be a reckoning, if he ever worked up enough nerve to come outside and face her. Now that I am older I understand. I didn't at the time. Maybe that was better.

Overall, celebration was a happy time. The memory is a pleasing one. It was a homecoming ... a ceremony ... a reward for getting through another year during a time when this was difficult to do.

It was good to have a celebration when a task is completed.

ANOTHER TIME

"Let There Be Light, and There Was Light ..."

But not until after Clenard came to our house.

> If they're alone and it is night,
>
> Some folks nearly die of fright.
>
> When light from wire replaced kerosene
>
> It really changed the country scene.

"Electrification of the family farm is the greatest advancement ever to take place in this country," a farmer friend once told me. This is likely a true statement. With the passage of time and additional thought, the truthfulness grows stronger.

After going through a modern holiday season, it is difficult to imagine that there ever was a time when there was no ready electricity. Appliances, TV, computers, dependable power for all our modern toys is a given. We don't even think about it. When ice knocks out our power for a time, we become irritable and unforgiving for the inconvenience.

Yet, it wasn't long ago, in the history of humankind, that electrical power was not available for everyone. Many of us seniors can remember when electricity came, but the last couple of generations cannot even imaging such a thing, let along remember life without it.

Electricity changed the basics. There was a small circle of light that stretched out from the kerosene lamp, or the lantern used when milking. That dull yellow glow was an improvement over candles and other earlier lighting systems. But electricity changed the color of our light to a whiter glow, and it chased those shadows that surround us much farther away. IT PUSHED THE SHADOWS FARTHER AWAY FROM HUMANKIND.

"Electricity can kill you." That was accepted then and remains true today. Then why don't birds get electrocuted when they land on power lines? There is much we don't know, but we accept certain truths because they work. Have you ever had an electrical leak?

Perhaps the odor of kerosene not being there was one of the early improvements made by electricity. Lamps and lanterns no longer had to be carried wherever light was needed. Those glass globes that kept the kerosene flames from blowing out no longer had to be cleaned of soot. Wicks no longer had to be trimmed to provide an even flame.

But the nature of our light itself was the greatest change. It was instant by flipping a switch. No adding fuel, lighting matches, adjusting the flame, just instant chasing shadows out of reach, with white light.

While the new power first invaded our cities and towns, farmers appreciated it when the connecting wires finally reached them because the first applications changed their work. Gasoline engines were acceptable for powering many farm needs, but there were others that were almost intended for the new power. Placing an electrical motor on the pump jack, replacing the windmill, was one of the earliest changes after electricity reached farms. The need for water was so basic, thus this application is logical as well as practical.

One farmer commented, "We bought a new milking machine shortly before electricity reached us. It was intended to operate by a gasoline engine until electricity arrived. Our frustration with the undependable habits of that gas engine drove us back to milking by hand until we got electricity the following year. The electrical motor operated the milker so well we were able to add more milk cows to our herd without increasing the chore schedule."

In many instances, the gasoline engines continued to provide farm power for many uses where it wasn't convenient to run wire; pumping water, washing clothes, buzzing fire wood, threshing grain, filling silo, and a host of other chores where such power was appropriate. People collect those engines today, and show them off at various events. They are still running when properly maintained. Of course, one can still light up a kerosene lantern and create shadows if desired, and many homes still have them hidden away, brought out if the electricity does fail.

Electricity did not arrive on most farms until the mid 1930s and 1940s. Some power companies established experimental farm lines. All kinds of electrical appliances were tested. This new power was used for grinding meat, for heating and cooling, for milking cows, cooking, and this was just the beginning. In those early days, electricity would cost the farmer about $2 per month after the initial cost of $50 to get the buildings wired for electricity. Getting the electrical service out to the farms was the biggest challenge and a number of electrical cooperatives developed to provide rural service.

It is likely that we still haven't heard the last of it, but early on farmers were opposed to the way the electrical lines were run through the fields. There was a hesitation about what that electrical power would do to people and animals as it went running down the wires. Of course, this concern was "poo pooed" by the power companies. This concern occurred again during the past couple of years. And it will likely come up again as our ability to test and measure ascends to the heights of our ability to manufacture and market.

It was about 1943 when Clenard Starks came to our house. He had attended a school and learned how to put this new "electricity" into houses, barns and buildings, hook everything together and make it all work ... it was a happening when he came. We were excited.

Clenard told us when the job would be completed. We prepared a celebration. Our family was there and Clenard's folks came to join us for supper under the new lights.

Clenard finished things up. Thought a minute, reached out and flipped the switch. NOTHING HAPPENED!

Actually, he had to go back to one of the boxes he had put in a wall, do something to it before he struck light. The shadows began disappearing immediately, and have continued to grow in impact ever since. The new lights in the barn changed the color of the milk from a beige to a white. That wire Clenard ran from the barn to the house back in 1943 has lost most of its covering, yet, if it is scraped, it is still a bright copper.

Will young people coming out of the holiday season with all kinds of modern pieces requiring electricity and batteries ever understand this world of before electricity? You might do an "eyes shut" experiment just to discover the sounds we live with that is converting electricity to a desired form in our homes constantly.

Electricity is one of those things that may be difficult to understand, but easy to accept, much like, "Why can you see more with your eyes closed than with them open?"

Electrification of the farm may well be the greatest influence on rural living in this century. Perhaps we only now remember the importance of this convenience when it is stopped by some ice or a tree limb. When power is restored, it is taken for granted instantly.

In those earliest days of electricity in the country, the power was often a part time thing. If there was any weather, wind, snow, rain, ice, whatever happened in nature could send us back into the darkness and shadows of another time.

In those early days, a number of companies sprouted up to provide electric service to the homes and farms. Some still exist, but many have disappeared into larger power sources.

We were the last farm on the end of the line serviced by the REA (Rural Electrification Association). Our next door neighboring farm was served by Consumers Power. They were the last hook-up on the Consumers' line.

Sometimes our power would go off, but we could see the lights on at the next farm. At other times, we would have lights and the view to the west would be dark. I doubt if anyone on that road can remember the last time they were without electrical power.

The companies providing electrical service today have certainly made us dependent on that service. Would you have it any other way?

Flowing Well

Fifty years ago, a strong stream of cold water came spurting out of that pipe, most of which was hidden beneath the ground ... only about four feet of it was visible. How long before that was it drilled? How far down does the buried pipe go? Who did this?

Yet today, that stream of water continues to pressure its way from deep within the earth to the surface creating its own small stream that runs down the grade to the ditch by the road, down the ditch to the small trout stream where it disappears into the larger flow. The streams travel as one through the woods and swamp, eventually joining with the larger river.

Will that flowing well run dry someday? Will it run like that forever? Perhaps we'll never know. That well has brought untold gallons of water out of the ground every minute ... every hour ... every day ... every week ... every month ... every year ... every decade.

What a miracle this would seem in the deserts of the world. What a waste of water it would seem to some.

Yet, in that rural green setting, by the edge of the woods, that flowing well continues to do its thing. Here in the midst of rivers and streams that never shut down, the well seems a natural part of the nature of things.

Slipping the hand under that flow of water, capturing enough of the cold flow to take a drink, remembering how long it has been waiting for this chance to help humankind, it seems that it is there for this single purpose, and that is good.

TREASURES FROM THEN

Discards from another time edge out of the cedars by the swamp, taking on a renewed value today.

That milk tank from the top of the long discarded separator is cocked against a rock, a reminder of when it held whole milk before it went through to become cream and skim, the latter fed to squealing pigs.

Bailing wire, once so plentiful, now discarded, is rusting away; a reminder that twine is relatively new. Before twine, that wire was used to fix everything from fences to exhaust systems. A way of life was altered when bailing wire gave way to twine.

A fender remains from a long ago pickup.

There are many boards from many things.

Harness straps with clinging rings and buckles accompany a pair of tugs not hooked to any load.

Remains of a childhood sled are parked alongside a wagon and tricycle, as the past is fused with today. A pump, once used to move liquid waste, deposited by female horses, into barrels for market, had some dull brass fittings resisting time.

A galvanized tub keeps company with the umbrella shaped heater top that kept little chicks warm until they could deal with the world on their own.

The flat tire from a wheelbarrow rests next to a tire pump that doesn't ... rocks and boards with bent, rusting nails, cluster with the rusting drive wheels of an ancient spreader.

All pieces of the past, important to the present, and the future. All tenses are intense.

Good Connections

"Tonkta, tonkta, tonkta, tonkta" was the sound made by the electric fence that was supposed to keep the cows and horses in the pasture but it was a temperamental thing.

When the ground was wet, it would really "tonkta" you if you made contact. While the ground was dry, not a great deal happened, but one hoped the cows would remember how it was when the grass was wet.

If a weed touched the wire someplace, it wouldn't "tonkta." There was a little red light bulb on the thing that was supposed to blink if a weed touched the wire. Sometimes it worked.

Once the light blinked, someone had to take the corn knife and walk the fence, cutting off any weeds that might be causing the problem. Other things could make the light blink, too.

Sometimes we would take pieces of grass and lay them on the fence. As the grass was slid closer to the wire, the smaller the distance between the fingers and the wire, the stronger the "tonkta."

Once when my cousin was visiting, she pointed to a piece of wire on the ground next to the fence and told me to lay that on the fence. I knew what it would do, so I wouldn't do it.

My little sister said, "I will" and grabbed the wire and touched the electric fence with it before we could stop her.

When the wire hit the fence, and the shock hit her fingers, she looked at me and said, "Stop that." Then she put the wire back on the fence and got another shock, and yelled "Stop that" again. She had tested that wire several times before we got her stopped so we could laugh.

Our Telephone

64-F-14 was our phone number. What this meant was that we were on line 64 and our ring was one long and four short rings. We could ring others on line 64 directly by cranking their rings, two long and three short, one long and two short, etc. When we cranked out a particular series on our line, it rang into every phone hooked into our party line 64.

This ringing alerted everyone with a phone that a conversation was going to begin and some of the more concerned party liners would listen in to hear calls where they were neither the caller or the callee. They were snoops!

However, if help was needed, one long ring notified everyone that someone was in trouble. Everyone on the line picked up and help was on the way.

When someone on another line, like 65, was called, a single ring was answered by "central" who then connected you to the other line and rang your party for you. "Central" later became "operator."

The telephone itself was a wooden box with a crank on the side, two bells on the top, a shelf and a mouthpiece on the front.

Each phone had a magneto inside. When the crank on one phone was turned, the bells on the other phones would ring from the electricity generated by turning the crank. Each phone had a place for two batteries, commonly referred to as telephone batteries. The batteries powered the magnets in the mouthpiece and the receiver so a two-way conversation resulted.

Later on, the individual phone batteries disappeared and the entire phone system was powered from the phone company. As technology developed, smaller party lines appeared, then two-party lines, and then to private lines.

From those early days when there might be two dozen families on a single line, the wait for the line to free up might be a long one, especially if a couple of long-winded phone subscribers got to solving all the world's problems while you were waiting to make a call.

Some of the more impatient users would suggest that people on the party line should not be allowed to have a chair by their phone.

Of course, those early phones had to be fastened to each other by two wires in order to work. Our phone cost us $4 to purchase in 1943. The idea of the "cell phone technology" was in the distant future. Then, the idea that wires could carry the voice from place to place was unreal. Actually, it still is.

NEIGHBOR ROY

He had always been there, Roy had. For half a century that I know of, and he was there before I was.

One of my photographs that became a magazine cover had a sparkling jewel in the early morning image. That jewel was a reflection of the window in Roy's barn, reflecting just as a good neighbor responds in time of need. Like a jewel, a good neighbor is a precious thing.

What does one remember of things past – catching a fly ball and running into their new fence. Once Roy had a cement block making machine in his yard. He made blocks and sold them. There were stacks of blocks in the barn until people came in trucks and hauled them away to building sites.

Roy and his family were neighbors since we moved there when I was four. When I discovered the ability to get lost in a book, they let me use theirs. They had a curved glass book case. The rules were that a book must be returned to the shelf as soon as it was finished.

The entire Covert family were our neighbors, not just Roy. Good neighbors are especially important in rural areas.

They had a TV set before we did. It was a treat to go there and watch this new entertainment. Before they brought their TV to the neighborhood, the only time I had seen one was downtown. Dad took me to town to see Joe Louis fight. There, pushed up to the front window of the radio shop, facing out so those in the street could see, was a tiny little rolling picture of the fight.

There was a large crowd of us out there, standing in the street in this small town, watching this latest demonstration of technology.

At this point, if there was sound to go with the picture, the radio, tuned to a station covering the event provided it. When Coverts got their TV, they had sound on their set.

Carol, my younger sister, recalls, "I had picked some wildflowers and was taking them to school to my teacher. I sat with Darlene Covert on the bus. She was so nice to me I gave the flowers to her instead of the teacher." Coverts were like that. They were people people. Folks liked them and they always had a lot of family and friends around.

Music was always important to all of us. Music and church involvement were lifelong activities. Coverts made the kind of music that seemed to come directly from the soul, using the human body as a tool to conduct the sound. Larry Covert was a little younger than I. Jerry, Darlene, and Gary were all younger. Darlene, and my sister Audrey were about the same age, and were always close friends.

Once when I was traveling to Boston, Darlene and her husband Gil, took me on a trip around the city. Gill was a history buff, and Boston is loaded with it. That was one of the most meaningful tourist excursions I have ever taken.

When Dad was sick, the Coverts were so generous with the use of their phone when we needed to place doctor calls that were uncomfortable to make from our house. There spirit of support and caring was that deeply rooted in old fashioned country values. At Dad's funeral, Roy came up to me and said, "Bud, Cecil was a good neighbor ... we are going to miss him ...." And that was all he was able to complete before additional speech became impossible for him. It was the highest compliment he could pay.

Although my relationship with the community and the people has not been close since leaving the area thirty years ago, there have always been waves and brief conversations when paths cross through the years.

Once, long ago, Ted Case brought his threshing machine, with his little Model T coupe hooked behind, to the Covert property to thresh grain. Going to Coverts for threshing dinner remains a good memory, although misty now.

The straw stack from the threshing stood just east of our driveway until the straw was gone.

It was not long ago when Roy and Fern celebrated their 50th wedding anniversary. Mother had informed us that we were expected to be there and would likely be called upon to sing. There was a great turnout in that small town where they had lived and raised their children.

All the Darnells were there, as instructed by Mother. Somehow the Darnells and Coverts ended up singing a couple of hymns. This was done without practice. Three or four decades after we had last sung together left some edges a little ragged.

After the songs were over, my brother said, "We must have sounded pretty bad. I saw tears in Roy's eyes." I am pleased that we did this. I'm also very pleased that Roy was touched.

Mother called this morning and said, "Roy died this morning."

I am sorry for his family and for those of us who must now live in this world without him. For those who cared for him during his illness, my prayers are with them as they now rest and regain their strength, and go on adjusting to a world without Roy.

And in closing, I repeat the words that Roy used, once upon a time, "He was a good neighbor."

HAZENS

Mike Hazen moved to the farm next to ours when we were in Miss Tompkins' fifth grade class. Mike and I chatted at our 45th high school class reunion last summer.

The Hazen Farm had a full-sized river running the length of it. All we had was a small spring fed creek that started a couple of hundred feet inside our east line fence, meandered through the cedar swamp, and finally dumped into Mike's river just beyond our west line fence. Because Mike had a full sized river, many of us were attracted to it.

The community swimming hole was beside Mike's house. While the water was cold, it was ten miles closer to us than the nearest lake that had warmer water. Youth seems more tolerant of cold than does maturity. Today I would insist on the lake for any water contact. In those days the river was fine ... even better than the lake because we didn't have to share it with so many other people.

Mike had other family too. He had a dad and mom, a sister and a brother, but they were all older. Mike and I became friends. We played on the same basketball and baseball teams, and when we played we didn't clutter up the school showcases with a bunch of gaudy trophies. Ours was not a talent that folks wanted to remember, but we played nonetheless.

Mike was always class president and I was proud to be his friend. We double dated, and eventually he married my cousin. We drove to Central Michigan University together for one semester, each of us driving the 30 miles every other day. We were lucky to get through that one semester on that program. We didn't force Central Michigan to show off any of our trophies either.

Many of the things we did were away from people so they didn't cause any problems with neighbors or law enforcement officials. It has always puzzled me as to how some things done in one place seem so different when done someplace else. We were good friends, a condition that is supportive to all participants, thus encouraging each to excel or exceed, depending on the circumstance.

Things that are area acceptable/unacceptable include throwing stones. Throwing is a natural urge, almost a need, humankind has been throwing since learning to walk in the bipod position. There is no harm when throwing a stone on the farm. Throw it as far, as high as hard as muscularly possible, and it is still not a problem.

Now take that same rock, the same boy, the same arm power, and place them in a highly populated area, and the kid instantly becomes an outlaw. When he throws that rock, it is likely to hit a window, a car, another person, and it makes a horrible noise if it hits a garbage can or someone's dog. Farm dogs are too suspicious to get caught by a boy with a rock.

Guns are another thing that get kids in trouble today. On the farm they were never a problem because they were tools for specific tasks just like a hammer, a shovel, fork, or any other tool. Take that tool into a different neighborhood and it can cause problems. Using the wrong tool for the wrong task will always be a problem. People need to be advised in the appropriate usage of all tools at all times. Mike and I would take our rifles to the woods and practice. Rural life was like that.

Town kids might make comments about some of the country odors brought to town on farm kids, but they didn't usually make such statements when country folks would hear them, or if they did they were in a group of town kids, and not making the observation as a single person.

As we progressed through school, it became evident that Mike was the more impressive scholar. He was a strong public speaker, confident and popular. We were both in the top 10 in our graduating class. Without Mike and I, the class would have had only 27 members, but we brought that total count up to only one short of 30. Mike was near the top of the top 10, I just made the count.

Together we participated in the junior and senior plays, and generally took ourselves seriously. Fortunately, the rest of the world was more objective.

While our farms had a common line fence, each farm got electricity from a different supplier. Hazens were on the west side of the bridge and they were supplied by Consumers Power. We were east of the bridge and REA (Rural Electric Association) provided us power. In those early days, electricity was not as dependable as it is today.

A little wind might stop the electrical flow. When our electricity would go off, the first thing we would do was go to the window and look westward to see if we could see any lights at Hazens. As time passed, other members of the Hazen family played a part in our lives. As an early adult, I worked in the shop near Mike's dad. When we were driving to Central, his sister lived in Mt. Pleasant and we often stopped in to see her and her daughter while we were between classes.

Mike's older brother and his wife were so helpful to Mother after Dad died. They kept an eye on things and he kept her driveway plowed in the winter, and proved to be a good neighbor. Good neighbors may take a lifetime to prove themselves. They are there when needed. About the greatest compliment that can be extended in the country is, "They were good neighbors."

Mike was always a good neighbor, more than that, he was a good friend. Likely because he never threw that stone or shot his gun in densely populated areas. That can make a difference.